W9-CFW-258

BE YOUR
★ BEST ★
YOU

BE BOLD!

A HERO'S GUIDE
TO BEING BRAVE

ELSIE OLSON

Consulting Editor, Diane Craig, M.A./Reading Specialist

Super Sandcastle

An Imprint of Abdo Publishing
abdobooks.com

abdobooks.com

Printed in the United States of America, North Mankato, Minnesota
052019
092019

THIS BOOK CONTAINS
RECYCLED MATERIALS

Design: Sarah DeYoung, Mighty Media, Inc.
Production: Mighty Media, Inc.
Editor: Jessica Rusick
Cover Photographs: iStockphoto; Shutterstock Images
Interior Photographs: iStockphoto; Mighty Media, Inc.; Shutterstock Images

Library of Congress Control Number: 2018966959

Publisher's Cataloging-in-Publication Data
Names: Olson, Elsie, author.
Title: Be bold!: a hero's guide to being brave / by Elsie Olson
Other title: A hero's guide to being brave
Description: Minneapolis, Minnesota : Abdo Publishing, 2020 | Series: Be your best you
Identifiers: ISBN 9781532119651 (lib. bdg.) | ISBN 9781532174414 (ebook)
Subjects: LCSH: Courage--Juvenile literature. | Bravery--Juvenile literature. | Heroism--Juvenile
    literature. | Self-confidence in children--Juvenile literature.
Classification: DDC 179.6--dc23

Super SandCastle™ books are created by a team of professional educators, reading specialists, and content developers around five essential components—phonemic awareness, phonics, vocabulary, text comprehension, and fluency—to assist young readers as they develop reading skills and strategies and increase their general knowledge. All books are written, reviewed, and leveled for guided reading, early reading intervention, and Accelerated Reader™ programs for use in shared, guided, and independent reading and writing activities to support a balanced approach to literacy instruction.

CONTENTS

BE YOUR BEST YOU!

Have you ever had something seem scary or weird? But then found the **courage** to face your fear?

Superheroes know boldness is cool. And they prove it at home, on the bus, and in school.

YOU HAVE THE POWER.
BE A HERO TOO.
BE BRAVE AND BE BOLD.

BE YOUR BEST
YOU!

WHAT IS BOLDNESS?

Being bold means having **courage**. People who are bold are brave or daring. They take chances. They try new things. People who are bold face their fears.

Are You Bold?

- Have you ever talked to a new kid at school?

- Have you ever stopped a friend from saying something mean?

- Have you admitted to making a mistake?

These are acts of boldness!

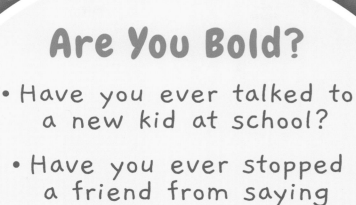

BE BOLD!

It's important to be brave. But true heroes are smart too. They don't take unnecessary risks. These are actions that could put themselves or others in danger. Superheroes also don't say things that could hurt others.

SUPERHEROES ON TV
SHOW BOLDNESS
BY SAVING THE WORLD
AND FACING BAD GUYS.

But kids like you have the superpowers to be bold too!

BABY STEPS

Superheroes show boldness in big ways. But being bold often starts small! When you're facing a scary task, break it into small parts. Face each small part one at a time. Then they won't seem so **overwhelming**.

FIVE SECONDS

It can be scary to do something brave. So use the five-second rule. Break up a scary task into five-second actions. Do them one at a time!

BE ADVENTUROUS

Your sense of adventure is a great superpower. This is your openness to new experiences.

Be adventurous by traveling to new places. Or try something you've never done before.

IT'S OKAY
IF YOU DON'T LIKE
SOMETHING RIGHT AWAY.
YOU MAY NEVER LIKE IT.

But you won't know unless you try!

LET YOURSELF FAIL

Making mistakes is another superpower to find your boldness. Mistakes happen all the time. Everyone makes them.

Superheroes know that it is okay to fail sometimes. They learn from their mistakes.

BE BOLD
AND
TRY THINGS
YOU AREN'T GOOD AT.

KNOW WHEN TO SAY NO

Being bold can mean saying yes to scary things. But knowing when to say no is a superpower too.

Heroes won't do something that could hurt others. They speak up when they see something wrong.

FIND YOUR MAGIC PHRASE

When you are afraid, a magic phrase can help. These are words special to you. They could be "I am brave." Or "I can do it." Repeat them to yourself.

This can give you courage!

DO YOUR RESEARCH

Boldness means **overcoming** fears. People are afraid of things for many different reasons. Sometimes it's because they don't understand something.

HEROES
FACE FEAR
BY LEARNING ABOUT WHAT THEY ARE AFRAID OF.

Once you learn more about something, you might realize it isn't so scary!

19

SUPERPOWER!

BELIEVE IN YOURSELF

Confidence is one of your greatest superpowers. It helps you be bold. You are **amazing**. There is no one quite like you!

NO TWO PEOPLE ARE EXACTLY ALIKE.

Your differences make you special. They are superpowers! How could you use them to be bold?

BE A HERO!

It's your turn to take a
stand. Act like a hero.
Lend a hand.

With the words you say
and the things you do,
be brave and be bold.
Be your best you!

WHAT WOULD YOU DO?

Being a hero is about making brave and bold choices. How would you use your superpowers in the situations below?

You're eating dinner at a friend's house, and her parents serve you something you've never eaten before.

There is a new kid in your classroom who needs a partner for a project.

You want to learn how to skateboard, but you are afraid of falling.

GLOSSARY

amazing – wonderful or surprising.

confidence – a feeling of faith in your own abilities.

courage – the strength to do something that is right, even if you are afraid.

overcome – to successfully face a problem or difficulty.

overwhelming – having a strong effect on your thoughts and feelings in a way that makes you feel like you can't do something.

ONLINE RESOURCES

Booklinks
NONFICTION NETWORK
FREE! ONLINE NONFICTION RESOURCES

To learn more about being bold and brave, visit **abdobooklinks.com** or scan this QR code. These links are routinely monitored and updated to provide the most current information available.